A WRINKLE IN TIME

by
Madeleine L'Engle

D1194546

Student Packet

Written by
Gloria Levine, M.A.

Contains masters for:

2	Prereading Activities
6	Vocabulary Activities
1	Study Guide
1	Art Activity
1	Math (Geometry) Activity
2	Critical Thinking Activities
1	Research Project
2	Writing Activities
1	Review Crossword
2	Comprehension Quizzes (Honors and Average)
2	Unit Exams (Honors and Average)

PLUS Detailed Answer Key

Note

The text used to prepare this guide was the Dell Yearling softcover published by Dell Publishing, ©1962 by Madeleine L'Engle. The page references may differ in other editions.

Please note: Please assess the appropriateness of this book for the age level and maturity of your students prior to reading and discussing it with your class.

ISBN 1-56137-498-9

Copyright infringement is a violation of Federal Law.

© 2000 by Novel Units, Inc., Bulverde, Texas. All rights reserved. No part of this publication may be reproduced, translated, stored in a retrieval system, or transmitted in any way or by any means (electronic, mechanical, photocopying, recording, or otherwise) without prior written permission from Novel Units, Inc.

Photocopying of student worksheets by a classroom teacher at a non-profit school who has purchased this publication for his/her own class is permissible. Reproduction of any part of this publication for an entire school or for a school system, by for-profit institutions and tutoring centers, or for commercial sale is strictly prohibited.

Novel Units is a registered trademark of Novel Units, Inc. Printed in the United States of America.

To order, contact your local school supply store, or—

Novel Units, Inc.
P.O. Box 97
Bulverde, TX 78163-0097

Web site: www.educyberstor.com

Name_____

Directions
Define and discuss the term "genre" with your class. Then complete the chart below based on your discussion.

Genre	Characters	Setting	Events	Examples
Realistic Fiction				
Fantasy				
Science Fiction				
Historical Fiction				
Non-Fiction				
Biography				

3

Name_____

Directions
Rate each of the following statements before you read the novel. Compare your ratings with a partner's, and discuss why you chose the particular ratings you did. (After you have completed the novel, discuss with your partner whether you would change any of the ratings.)

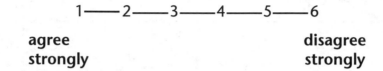

agree
strongly

disagree
strongly

Freedom of Choice Opinionnaire

_____ 1. It will be good when someday people are more alike.

_____ 2. Often the negative things in people's lives are caused by bad luck.

_____ 3. Most people get their just desserts.

_____ 4. There is no such thing as evil; bad things happen because people make mistakes.

_____ 5. It's a good idea to try to find the happy medium.

_____ 6. What will be, will be.

_____ 7. Success is usually a matter of being in the right place at the right time.

_____ 8. In life, you should protect yourself by reducing the risks you take.

_____ 9. Some people are just born no good.

_____ 10. Usually you should stop fighting, for it will only make things worse.

_____ 12. It is better to plan your actions than to trust in "fate."

_____ 13. If you don't try, you will never know if you can succeed.

_____ 14. If you look hard enough, you will find some good in everyone.

_____ 15. Where there is a will, there is a way.

_____ 16. The only way to deal with something deadly serious is to treat it lightly.

Name_____

Chapter 1

As you read Chapter 1, think about why Meg is having such a rough time.

1. What is the weather like as the story opens? How does that "set the tone"?

2. What are your impressions of Meg? What sort of student is she? Why? Would she be a friend of yours?

3. Why does Meg get into a fight with one of the boys on the way home from school?

4. Why are people gossiping about the Murrys? How is Mrs. Murry's reaction to the gossip different from Meg's?

5. Who is Charles Wallace and how is he different from most little boys?

6. What do Meg's parents do for a living?

7. Who comes to visit the Murrys? Where did Charles meet her before?

8. How does Meg seem to feel about the visitor? Why do you think she reacts that way?

9. How can you tell that Mrs. Murry is shocked by something the visitor says? Why is she shocked?

10. List three problems Meg has.

Charles Wallace has an almost "uncanny" understanding of his sister, Meg. Who understands you the best? Give some examples of times when that person seemed to know how you felt or what you were up to—without your saying anything.

Chapter 2

As you read Chapter 2, try to picture the story unfolding—as if there is a movie being shown in your mind.

1. Who is Mrs. Who? What is she like? What is unique about her?

2. What does Dennys mean when he tells Meg she should "use a happy medium"? Do you agree?

3. How does Meg end up in the principal's office? How did Mrs. Whatsit's visit set off the chain of events that results in Meg's problem with the principal?

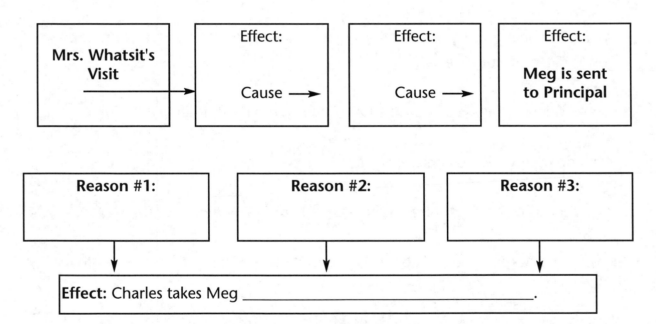

4. Where does Charles take Meg? What reasons does he have?

5. Whom do Meg and Charles find hanging around the "haunted house"? Why is he there?

6. Why did Mrs. Whatsit take Mrs. Buncombe's sheets?

7. What do Charles and Meg invite Calvin to do?

Sketch Mrs. Who as you imagine her to look:

Chapter 3

As you read Chapter 3, see what you can learn about Meg's father and the trouble he is in.

1. How is Mrs. Murry different from Calvin's mother?

Mrs. Murry	Calvin's mother

2. How is Meg able to help Calvin with his homework? What does this show about her ability?

3. Why doesn't Meg get better grades in math?

4. Why does Calvin "quiz" Meg? What does he learn about her, as a result?

5. Why does Calvin say he feels as if he were "just being born"? (p. 44)

6. How does Meg's mother respond when Meg asks her to explain a "tesseract"? Why do you think she reacts that way?

7. What does Meg know about her father's disappearance?

8. Why does Mrs. Who say to Mrs. Whatsit, "An old ass knows more than a young colt"? (p. 54)

Meg's mother talks about how special Charles is. Briefly describe the most unique person you know. Does that person's uniqueness cause him or her any problems?

Chapter 4
As you read Chapter 4, try to "hear" the sounds described.

1. Who is Mrs. Which and what is she like?

2. On what sort of "trip" do Mrs. Who, Mrs. Whatsit, and Mrs. Which take the three children? Why? To what could you compare Meg's feelings during the trip?

3. Why does Mrs. Who speak in quotations?

4. What is Uriel like?

5. What does it mean to tesser?

6. How does Mrs. Whatsit change?

7. How do Meg, Charles, and Calvin use the flowers?

8. What is the "Black Thing"? How does Meg feel as she looks at the "Black Thing"?

9. Why do you think the three young people have been taken to see the "Black Thing"?

What sort of music do you imagine coming from the throats and wings of the magical creatures? (p. 66)

Chapter 5

As you read Chapter 5, think about other stories and movies you are reminded of.

1. What do the pictures on pages 76 and 77 have to do with the story?

2. Who is the Cheshire Cat and why does Mrs. Who remind Meg of that cat? (p. 79)

3. What sort of mistake does Mrs. Whatsit make when she "tessers" the three young people? What effect does that mistake have on them?

4. Why do the travelers stop on the belt of Orion?

5. What is the "Happy Medium" like? Why is her name appropriate?

6. What does the Happy Medium show the young people? Why?

7. What do Gandhi, Copernicus, and the other people listed on page 89 have in common?

Rank the people listed below from 1-5 (1=the person who has been the greatest fighter for truth, beauty, and goodness). Be ready to defend your answers.

__Gandhi	__Copernicus	__ da Vinci	__Shakespeare
__Pasteur	__Buddha	__Beethoven	__Rembrandt
__St. Francis	__Mme. Curie	__Bach	__Einstein
__Schweitzer	__Martin Luther King		

Mrs. Which tells the young people that they will "fight the powers of darkness." In what other stories does such a fight go on? If you were to look through the past month's newspapers, what specific examples of that fight might you find?

Chapter 6

As you read Chapter 6, think about how the author builds suspense.

1. What did Mrs. Whatsit used to be? What happened to her?

2. How do the young people see their mothers?

3. Mrs. Which doesn't think it is a good idea to let the young people see their mothers. How does she turn out to be right?

4. When the young people first land on Camazotz, what do they see?

5. What "little talisman" does Mrs. Whatsit give each of the three young people? What talisman do you suppose she would give you?

6. What does Mrs. Who give Meg to use on Camazotz?

7. What instructions does Mrs. Which give the children before they go into the town?

8. What is odd about the people on Camazotz?

9. To whom do the young people talk? How does the mother react? Does she remind you of anyone you have met in other books or in movies?

10. What is the paper boy like? What does he reveal?

11. Describe Calvin's premonition.

What questions does this chapter raise in your mind?

Chapter 7

As you read Chapter 7, think about what the man with the red eyes represents. Ask yourself: What is his message? What's wrong with that message? In the real world, where do I hear his "message"?

1. Meg thinks that Charles Wallace is "whistling in the dark" when he makes a joke about jam (p. 117). What does that expression mean?

2. How does the man with the red eyes communicate with Meg and the others?

3. What does the man with the red eyes offer Charles Wallace and the others?

4. Why does Charles Wallace hit the man with the red eyes? What is the result?

5. How does Charles keep the man from hypnotizing the others? What would you recite, in their situation? Why isn't he as successful in protecting himself in the end?

6. Why does Meg tackle Charles Wallace? What is the result?

7. What sort of dinner does the man give the young people? How do they differ in their enjoyment of the taste? Why?

This story was written in 1962. What was the world political situation like at that point? What threats did the U.S. face? What similarity do you see between those threats and the ones posed by the man with the red eyes?

Add other names to the list of "evildoers" below and rank them from 1-5 (1=most vicious, immoral person).

__Ivan the Terrible   __Hitler   __Caligula   __ Genghis Khan

__ _____   __ _____   __ _____   __ _____

__ _____   __ _____   __ _____   __ _____

Chapter 8

As you read Chapter 8, think about the differences between being "alike" and being "equal."

1. How has Charles Wallace changed? Why?

2. How does Calvin try to help Charles Wallace return to normal? Is he successful?

3. The evil forces try to get at the young people by shaking their trust in people. Find two examples.

4. Why is the little boy screaming? What do you suppose he will be like the next day?

Do you agree with the hypnotized Charles Wallace that "differences create problems"? When do you want to be the same as everyone else? When do you want to be different? Do you ever pretend to be the same when you are really different?

Chapter 9

As you read Chapter 9, look for how Meg and Calvin use their gifts. Look for signs that Meg is losing faith.

1. Where is Mr. Murry? How has he changed?

2. Why does Calvin tell Charles Wallace that he is like Ariel (p. 147)?

3. How does Meg get to her father? How does he react to being with her?

4. How does Meg use Mrs. Who's glasses once she is in the column?

5. How do Meg and her father get out of the column?

6. What is "IT"? How does Meg follow Mrs. Whatsit's advice to "use her anger"?

7. How does Meg argue against the idea that everyone on Camazotz is "equal"?

8. How does Meg's father try to help her solve the problem of how to resist being absorbed into IT?

If you were in Meg's shoes, what would you recite to help yourself concentrate so that you wouldn't be hypnotized? What else might you do to avoid having your mind controlled? Can you think of other stories where mind control plays a part?

Chapter 10
As you read Chapter 10, look for reasons why Meg is disappointed in her father and think about a time when you felt somewhat the same way.

1. How is Meg injured?

2. How does Meg feel about her father's tessering them? Have you ever felt similar feelings about one of your parents, when they were trying to do what they thought was right?

3. Where do Meg and the others end up when Mr. Murry "tessers" them?

Chapter 11
As you read Chapter 11, see how Meg's initial feelings of alarm change.

1. How do the beasts help Meg?

2. If you were responsible for staging the scene described in this chapter, what sort of costume would you make for Aunt Beast? What pieces of music would you use for the background music?

3. Why do the beasts think that it is a limiting thing to have the ability to see?

4. How do Meg and Aunt Beast feel about each other?

5. What problem do Meg and the others face?

6. How do the Beasts help Meg and the others plan what to do? Why won't they allow Mr. Murry to return to Camazotz?

7. How can you tell that creatures on Ixchel communicate with beings on other planets?

In communicating with Meg and the others, Aunt Beast suggests that Meg should stop trying to find words to describe Mrs. Whatsit and just concentrate on what she is. Try concentrating on what something is—not on words that describe it: a piece of pizza, your best friend, love....How successful are you?

Chapter 12

As you read Chapter 12, think about how the ending is like the ending of other quest stories you know.

1. Why is it Meg who has to save Charles Wallace—not Calvin or Mr. Murry? What do you think would happen if Mr. Murry were allowed to return to Camazotz?

2. How does Meg feel about going back to Camazotz?

3. Why does Mrs. Whatsit compare life to a sonnet? What is her point?

4. What gift does Mrs. Whatsit give Meg before she returns to Camazotz?

5. How does Meg use the gift to conquer IT?

6. How has Meg changed Camazotz and how has Camazotz changed her? What do you suppose Camazotz is like after she leaves? What do you suppose Meg's life is like a month after the end of the story?

How is this story like other "quest" stories you may know—say, The Legend of the Holy Grail *or* The Dark Is Rising?

Directions

One partner draws dotted lines around two words in each group that are opposite in meaning. The other partner draws solid lines around the two words in each group that are similar in meaning.

Vocabulary List
frenzied 3
wraith-like 3
serenity 5
uncanny 5
subsided 7
vulnerable 8
prodigious 11
moderation 12
repulsive 13
exclusive 13
indignantly 17
pathetic 17
vigorously 19
intoned 19
supine 20
agility 20
relinquished 20
frivoling 21
unceremoniously 23
piteous 23
avid 26
ferocious 26
belligerent 26
antagonistic 27
tractable 27
sagely 29
inadvertently 30
indignation 31
disillusion 32
sport 32
compulsion 32
peremptory 36

1. requisition   agitation   compulsion
   serenity   perspective   equanimity

2. controlled   wraith-like   peremptory
   frenzied   piteous   authoritarian

3. disillusion   abdicate   relinquish
   subside   intone   amplify

4. impervious   uncanny   repulsive
   alluring   prodigious   invulnerable

5. sport   half-heartedly   sagely
   vigorously   agility   suppleness

6. belligerent   intractable   frivoling
   embracing   exclusive   pathetic

7. avid   prone   inimical
   antagonistic   supine   unceremoniously

Directions

A. Form a group of three. Pick a card and read the clue on it to the others in your group. Together, figure out the mystery words. Look at the vocabulary box only if you have to.

Set #1:

a tadpole does it	four-syllable verb that rhymes with a synonym for "selected"	from a word with the Greek suffix "osis": action, process

Set #2:

This doesn't mean wagered or bet.	capered; related to the French word for leg, *jambe*	two syllables, rhymes with a word that means "wandered"

Set #3:

related to the French word *marais,* meaning "marsh"	a bog	noun describing a type of ground or feeling that pulls you down

Set #4:

a scar is not this	a fly and a feeling might both be this	from the Greek word *hemera,* meaning "a day"

B. Divide the remaining words with other groups and make additional clue cards.

assimiliate 37	gamboled 38	retort 39	wryly 40
somber 40	indignant 40	legible 43	decipher 43
megaparsec 43	function 44	limitations 46	essence 47
dubiously 47	dappled 49	morass 49	classified 50
tangible 51	contradicted 53	instinctively 53	wafted 55
plaintively 55	deft 55	corporeal 57	elliptic 58
ineffable 59	ephemeral 61	muted 64	flanks 64
exaltation 64	centaur 64	metamorphose 65	infinity 66
monoliths 66	resonant 67	incomprehensible 68	obscure 71
corona 73			

illuminating 78	dissolution 79	intolerable 80
materialize 81	substantial 81	protoplasm 81
transition 84	reverberated 86	anticlimax 93
facet 93	ambrosia 94	nectar 94
eon 98	malignant 99	precipitously 99
sumac 99	propitious 100	talisman 100
simultaneously 103	furtive 104	aberration 106

A. Form two teams of 3 or 4 people each. A player from **Team A** picks one of the vocabulary words out of a hat or other container and either makes a drawing or acts out the word charades-style. His or her teammates try to guess the word within three minutes. After time is up, a person from **Team B** picks a vocabulary word out of the hat, and draws or acts it out for his or her teammates. A correct guess earns two points. The team with the greatest number of points at the end wins.

B. Write the vocabulary word that matches each definition or synonym, below.

1. _____ hurtful, malevolent
2. _____ skulking, stealthy
3. _____ charm, object of good luck
4. _____ concurrently, at the same time
5. _____ change
6. _____ lighting
7. _____ unbearable
8. _____ irregularity
9. _____ suddenly
10. _____ favorable, fortunate

Directions

Below is the journey that Meg, Charles, and Calvin must take to save Mr. Murry. As in many quests, they are not sure exactly what they will find or where they will go. Each time they come to a word along the way, look in the crystal ball for its synonym. Place the synonym in the space provided and proceed in this manner until the goal is reached. As you copy each synonym, also circle any shadowed letters in the word. When you reach the goal, place the shadowed letters in the blanks provided and discover where the travelers—like most characters on a quest—finally end up.

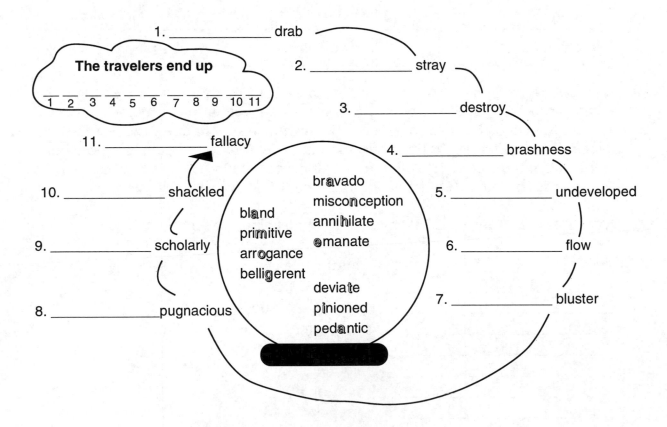

Name_____

A Wrinkle in Time
Activity #7: **Vocabulary**
Chapter 9
(**Note:** This activity has two pages.)

placidly 146	menacing 149	gibberish 150	myopic 153
insolent 153	defer 154	angular 156	ominous 156
inexorable 157	dais 157	disembodied 158	nauseating 158
systole 159	diastole 159	miasma 159	formaldehyde 161
cerebrum 161	cerebellum 161		

Acrostic

Find the missing word for each clue on the list above. Write the letters of the word in the space above the numbers. Then write each letter in the box having the same number inside the transparent column. A message from Father will appear.

TRANSPARENT COLUMN

__ __ __ __ __ __ __ __ __ __ __ __ __ __ __ __ __ __ __ __
1 2 3 4 5 6 7 8 9 10 11 12 13 14 15 16 17 18 19 20

__ __ __ __ __ __ __ __ __ __ __ __ __ __ __ __ __ __ __ __
21 22 23 24 25 26 27 28 29 30 31 32 33 34 35 36 37 38 39 40

Message: _____

Clues

1. chemical used to preserve specimens

Words

__ __ __ __ __ __ __ __ **H** __ __ __
19 7 9 25 24 2 14 10   6 14 10

2. poisonous mist

__ __ __ __ __ __
25 23 21 4 25 21

3. pointed, not curved

__ __ __ __ __ __ __
24 31 34 29 2 24 26

4. calmly

P __ __ __ __ __ __ __
   2 24 1 23 14 2 6

5. intangible, incorporeal

__ __ __ __ __ **B** __ __ __ __ __
14 23 13 5 25   15 14 23 5 14

6. inevitable, ceaseless

__ __ __ **X** __ __ __ **B** __ __
32 16 5   3 30 24   2 5

(more clues, next page)

Clues

Words

7. foreboding, spooky

‗ ‗ ‗ ‗ ‗ ‗ ‗
17 25 23 16 17 8 13

8. bold, rude

‗ ‗ ‗ ‗ ‗ ‗ ‗ ‗
23 16 13 17 2 20 33 18

9. threatening

‗ ‗ ‗ ‗ ‗ ‗ ‗ ‗
25 5 16 21 1 23 16 34

10. nonsense prattle

‗ ‗ **B B** ‗ ‗ ‗ ‗ **H**
34 23   12 22 23 13

11. nearsighted

‗ ‗ ‗ **P** ‗ ‗ ‗
25 11 39   23 1

12. having to do with pressure
    of blood as it is forced through
    the heart

‗ ‗ ‗ ‗ ‗ ‗ ‗
 4 38 4 28 36 2 27

13. acquiesce, accede, yield

‗ ‗ ‗ ‗ ‗
14 5 35 5 37

14. part of the brain responsible for
    conscious thought

‗ ‗ ‗ ‗ **B** ‗ ‗ ‗
1 5 9 5   9 40 25

Name_____

A Wrinkle in Time
Activity #8: **Vocabulary**
Chapters 10-12
(**Note:** This activity has two pages.)

atrophied 164	disintegration 167	corrosive 171	omnipotent 172
fallible 172	indentations 173	tentacles 174	tremor 177
trepidation 177	acute 178	counteracted 179	pungent 180
relinquish 180	perplexity 181	opaque 181	jeopardize 183
converged 187	despondency 188	distraught 189	reverberated 191
appallingly 193	formidably 195	ministrations 195	imperceptibly 203
permeating 205	reiterating 206	unadulterated 207	animated 208
catapulted 210			

Directions
Complete each statement with a word from the box above.

1. The little boy liked to pretend that he was an __ __ __ __ __ __ __ __ __ __
   king who made all the rules for everyone.　　　16　　　17　　　　18

2. Noting the delicious aroma __ __ __ __ __ __ __ __ __ __ the kitchen, Sam
   　　　　　　　　　　　　　25　　　　20
   called out, "Is there any popcorn left?"

3. She'd been fearless during the food fight, but when she saw the principal she was
   suddenly filled with __ __ __ __ __ __ __ __ __ __ __ __.
   　　　　　　　　12

4. He assured his customers that all the foods were pure and __ __ __ __ __ __
   __ __ __ __ __ __, with no additives or preservatives.
   7　　　　　　　15

5. After a moment of silence, the orator's powerful voice rolled __ __ __ __ __ __ __ __
   __ __ across the chamber.　　　　　　　　　　23　　　　13

6. Children think at first that their parents are perfect, but they soon learn that all
   adults are __ __ __ __ __ __ __ __.
   　　　　22

7. If you __ __ __ __ __ __ __ __ __ __ __ your hold on my coat, I will stop pulling your
   hair.　　　　　　　　　　1　2

8. The senator did not want to __ __ __ __ __ __ __ __ __ __ his chances for
                                                9   6   3

   re-election by supporting the unpopular measure.

9. The wet cat looked like a goner, but soon responded to the old man's kind

   __ __ __ __ __ __ __ __ __ __ __ __ __.
    11 14   5   21

10. Theo disliked the __ __ __ __ __ __ __ odor of the lotion, but he disliked getting
                                     10

    bitten by mosquitoes even more.

Notice the numbers under some of the letters you have written. Place the correct letter with its matching number on each line below to complete the thought.

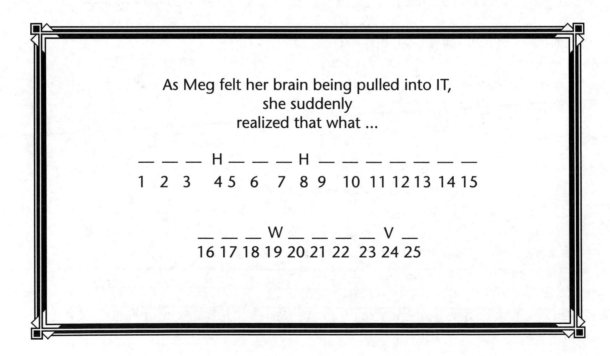

As Meg felt her brain being pulled into IT,
she suddenly
realized that what ...

__ __ __ H __ __ __ H __ __ __ __ __ __ __
1 2 3   4 5 6   7 8 9   10 11 12 13 14 15

__ __ __ W __ __ __ __ V __
16 17 18 19 20 21 22 23 24 25

Directions
Both of the science topics below are touched upon somewhere in the novel, *A Wrinkle in Time*. Form a group of three and choose one of the topics. Each student should use a different resource to look up information about the topic and summarize findings on the chart. Then cut out and glue all information to a posterboard to make a master chart, and use it to share findings with the class.

Topic: ESP (extra-sensory perception)

Source:_____

What it is: _____
_____

Some experiments and results: _____
_____
_____

Other information:_____
_____

- -

Topic: hypnosis (mind control)

Source:_____

What it is: _____
_____

Some experiments and results: _____
_____
_____

Other information:_____
_____
_____

Tesselations are repeating shapes that can fill a plane without leaving any spaces. Here is an example:

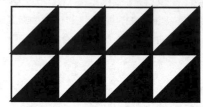

Notice that the square has the same area after it has been altered.

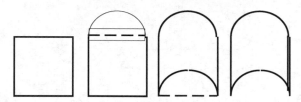

Here is a tessellation based on the altered square:

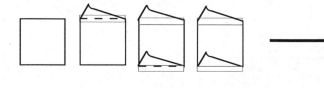

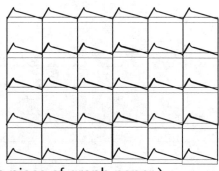

Color in alternating shapes in the tesselation at the right.

Make your own tesselation (You might want to use a piece of graph paper.)

Step 1: Alter a triangle, rectangle, or square so that it has the same area as the original.
Step 2: Fill the paper by repeating the altered shape.
Step 3: Color in alternating shapes.

Directions
Each of the places on the chart is one of the settings found in *A Wrinkle in Time*.
1. Form a group of three or four and choose a group recorder.
2. Brainstorm ideas about each place, based on the novel and on your own imaginations.
3. The group recorder jots down your ideas on the chart.
4. Together, create a travel brochure advertising one of the four locations. Include a map and other illustrations as well as information from your brainstorming chart.

Place: Murrys' hometown	**Place:** Uriel
Location:	**Location:**
Climate:	**Climate:**
Attractions:	**Attractions:**
History:	**History:**
Place: Camazotz	**Place:** Ixchel
Location:	**Location:**
Climate:	**Climate:**
Attractions:	**Attractions:**
History:	**History:**

Name_____

Directions

Mrs. Who speaks in quotes. Put each of the quotes, below, in your own words and explain why Mrs. Who speaks the quote when she does. Then use a book of quotations (like *Bartlett's Familiar Quotations*) to find ANOTHER quote she might have used to convey a similar idea.

1. **Quote:** "The heart has its reasons whereof reason knows nothing." (Pascal, p. 35)
   Paraphrase:

   Why Mrs. Who says this:

   Another Quote:

2. **Quote:** "Nothing deters a good man from doing what is honorable." (Seneca, p. 36)
   Paraphrase:

   Why Mrs. Who says this:

   Another Quote:

3. **Quote:** "The work proves the craftsman." (anonymous German, p. 64)
   Paraphrase:

   Why Mrs. Who says this:

   Another Quote:

4. **Quote:** "I do not know everything; still many things I understand." (Goethe, p. 101)
   Paraphrase:

   Why Mrs. Who says this:

   Another Quote:

Directions

In stories, the plot often is carried along by the causes and effects of decisions made by the characters. Had the characters made an alternate decision, the plot would have turned in a different direction. Even small decisions can bring about later events. We know this is also true in our own lives where decisions have real consequences.

A. Choose one of the following scenarios.

1) When Meg meets Calvin, she decides he is not to be trusted.
2) Meg and Charles decide to tell their mother about their plans to go with the three women in search of Mr. Murry.
3) Calvin decides that the sense of danger is too great to allow the others to enter the CENTRAL Central Intelligence Office.
4) Meg decides that it isn't time to use the spectacles yet when she sees her father in the column.
5) Charles Wallace decides that he won't ever look at the man with the red eyes so that he cannot be hypnotized.
6) Mr. Murry gives up to IT before the children arrive.
7) Mr. Murry decides not to try tessering his children.
8) Mr. Murry decides not to trust the "beasts" with his daughter.
9) Mr. Murry decides not to let Meg go back to Camazotz alone
10) Meg decides at the end that she will try to give love to IT.

B. Fill in the chart below to show what happens in the original scene—and what MIGHT have happened.

Situation: _____

Decision in Story	Alternate Decision
_____	_____
_____	_____
Results	**Results**
_____	_____
_____	_____

C. Write the alternate scene.

Name_____

A Wrinkle in Time
Activity #14: **Review Crossword**
(**Note:** Clues are on following page.)

Directions

Use the clues on the following page to solve the puzzle below.

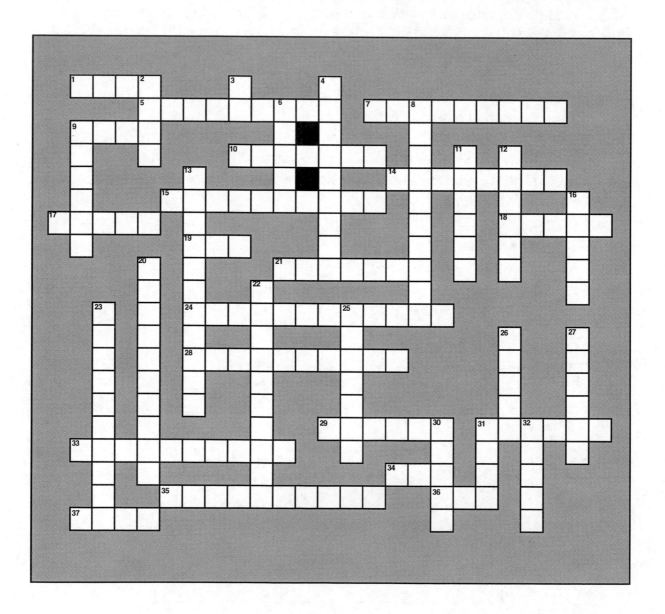

ACROSS

1. Aunt Beast has no ____.
5. The principal told Meg she should be more_____ in order to get better grades.
7. The enormous room where the children meet the man with the red eyes is lined with large _____.
9. Meg finds that this vanquishes IT.
10. The youngest of the three women.
14. The planet where Mr. Murry is trapped.
15. Meg's dog
17. The Dark Thing casts a _____shadow of evil over the earth.
18. This is the third planet from the star Malek, from which Meg and the others first view the Dark Thing.
19. She thinks she is ugly, but Calvin disagrees.
21. Meg and her mother grew worried when these stopped coming.
24. The capital city of Camazotz is where CENTRAL Central _____ is.
28. On Camazotz, no one suffers; it is customary to _____ anyone who becomes ill.
29. one of Meg's twin brothers
31. Mrs. Who took Mrs. Buncombe's ____.
33. Mrs. Who speaks in these.
34. Mrs. _____ calls Charles "Charlesie" and Meg "Megsie."
35. Calvin plays this.
36. The man with the _____eyes tells Charles and the others that it is easiest to submit to IT.
37. Mrs. Whatsit was once one of these.

DOWN

2. Mrs. Murry made this over a bunsen burner.
3. ____gains power over Charles.
4. The _____ is a concept having to do with the fifth dimension.
6. IT is a disembodied _____.
8. One of Mr. Murry's nicknames for Meg.
9. The author is Madeleine _____.
11. Charles trusts him and includes him as "one of us."
12. Mr. Murry is trapped in a transparent _____.
13. Mrs. Whatsit gave Calvin the gift of strengthening his ability to _____.
16. Aunt _____ cared for Meg after her father tessered her.
20. Mr. and Mrs. Murry were both _____.
22. Mrs. Whatsit tells Charles Wallace his gift is the _____ of childhood.
23. Charles knew his mother liked this and cheese on a sandwich.
25. Mrs. Who gives Meg her _____.
26. Mrs. ____ is the oldest and wisest of the three women.
27. Mrs. Whatsit gives Meg the gift of her _____.
30. Calvin calls Charles "old _____."
31. The turkey dinner tastes like this to Charles Wallace.
32. Meg shouts at IT that "like" and _____ are not the same thing.

Name_____

Directions
Label each statement **T** for True or **F** for False.

___1. The people in the town where the Murrys lived believe that Charles Wallace is below-average in intelligence.

___2. Charles Wallace's parents refuse to believe that he is any different from other children.

___3. Meg likes being considered "different" at school.

___4. Meg's teachers like her because she is an excellent student, like her brothers.

___5. Meg's parents are both teachers.

___6. Meg's mother is a beautiful scientist.

___7. Calvin is an excellent student from a large happy family.

___8. Charles looks into Calvin's eyes and decides that Calvin can be trusted.

___9. Meg thinks that Calvin is funny-looking, but doesn't say so.

___10. Mrs. Whatsit takes the young people to see the light cast over the earth, and they are comforted by it.

___11. The Happy Medium is never troubled by anything and refuses to allow others to be.

___12. The young people learn that their father is trapped on Camazotz where he has been trying to fight the Dark Thing.

___13. Most of the inhabitants of Camazotz act something like robots.

___14. One little boy invites Charles Wallace to play ball.

___15. Calvin senses that it is dangerous to go into the CENTRAL Central Intelligence Office.

Directions
Answer each question in one complete sentence.

1. Why do many people cluck in sympathy for Charles Wallace?

2. How do Charles Wallace's parents seem to feel about the fact that he is "different"?

3. Why does Meg get into conflicts with other students?

4. What do Meg's teachers seem to think of her?

5. What do the townspeople say about Mr. Murry's absence?

6. What is Mr. Murry's occupation?

7. What is Calvin's family life like?

8. What do Calvin and Charles Wallace have in common?

9. What opinion does Meg express to Calvin about his looks?

10. What does Mrs. Whatsit take the young people on her back to see?

11. What does the Happy Medium show the young people with her crystal ball?

12. What do the young people learn about what has happened to Mr. Murry?

13. How do the people of Camazotz act?

14. Why do Meg and the others notice one little boy on Camazotz?

15. How does Calvin feel about going into the Central Central Intelligence Office?

© Novel Units, Inc.

31

Identification
Find a character on the right who matches the description on the left. Write the letter of the character next to the matching number. Each character is to be used only once.

__ 1. one of the Murry twins
__ 2. Meg's little brother
__ 3. the person who rescues Charles Wallace
__ 4. Meg's beautiful and intelligent mother
__ 5. She speaks in quotations.
__ 6. She can change into a beautiful creature with wings.
__ 7. Calvin's mother
__ 8. He has a special ability to communicate.
__ 9. She's the oldest and wisest of the three women.
__10. He was trapped on Camazotz while fighting the Dark Thing.
__11. Her tentacles may look strange, but she cares lovingly for Meg.
__12. This brain controls the minds on Camazotz.
__13. He hypnotizes Charles.
__14. She has a crystal ball.

A. Meg
B. Charles Wallace
C. Dennys
D. Mrs. Murry
E. Calvin
F. Mr. Murry
G. Mrs. Whatsit
H. Mrs. Who
I. Mrs. Which
J. the Happy Medium
K. the Man with the Red Eyes
L. IT
M. Mrs. O'Keefe
N. Aunt Beast

Fill-Ins
Fill in each blank with the correct word or phrase.

Meg's (1.) _____ had been doing experiments involving the fifth dimension, known as the (2.) _____, when he mysteriously disappeared. Meg, her brother Charles Wallace, and their new friend Calvin go in search of Mr. Murry, who had been working on a secret project for the (3.) _____. Three mysterious women appear to assist them in their search: Mrs. (4.) _____, who used to be a star, Mrs. (5.) _____, who has trouble finding her own words, and Mrs. (6.) _____ who has trouble materializing completely. Charles Wallace meets Mrs. Whatsit in a nearby "haunted house" and soon realizes that she is the (7.) "_____" who stole Mrs. Buncombe's sheets. This strange little woman shows up at the Murry house during a (8.) _____ and shocks Mrs. Murry by telling her (9.) "_____ do exist." Charles Wallace takes Meg to the haunted house, where they meet (10.) _____ hanging around outside. Soon all three young people are on their way to a friendly planet where they learn that Mr. Murry is being held prisoner on (11.) _____. That planet had given in to the Power of Darkness, a giant black (12.) _____ that stands for evil. The Happy Medium allows the children to look through her (13.) _____ _____at Earth, which is partly covered by a (14.) _____ . She also lets them take a peek at a worried Mrs. Murry sitting in her (15)._____ and a harried Mrs.(16.) _____ whacking her children. The women then tesser the children to Camazotz where people act like (17.) _____, all doing the same things together. Charles Wallace tries to overcome the man with the (18.) _____ _____, the coordinator of the (19.) _____ Central Intelligence Building. Unfortunately Charles Wallace becomes (20.) _____ and tries to convince Meg and Calvin to give in. Using Mrs. Who's (21.) _____, Meg is able to pass through a transparent (22.) _____ that is trapping her father. The young people learn that a pulsating (23.) _____, called IT, controls everyone on Camazotz. IT nearly brainwashes Meg, but (24.) _____ saves her by tessering her to Ixchel. Because he is not expert at tessering, Meg suffers from the (25.) _____during the trip. Fortunately, Aunt (26.) _____ nurses Meg back to health. This tentacled creature has no (27.) _____, but Meg soon learns that you don't need them for understanding and love. Meg is angry with (28.) _____ at first for failing to save Charles Wallace. Then the three women show up, and help Meg see that only she has the power to do that. They don't tell her what that power is, but she learns when she returns to (29.) _____. what it is. She rescues Charles Wallace when she understands that she has the power of (30.)_____—which destroys the evil of IT.

Written Response

I. Analysis

Directions
Choose A or B and indicate the letter of the question you decide to answer.

A. Explain the main problem faced by the three young people and describe how they solve it. List at least three steps they take to achieve their goal.

B. Compare and contrast the three young people in the story. How are Meg, Calvin, and Charles Wallace alike? How are they different? Which one is most like you?

II. Critical and Creative Thinking

Directions
Choose C or D

C. "You should try for the happy medium."
Do you think the book supports this idea or contradicts it?
Back up your opinion with at least three examples from the story.

D. Pretend that you are Charles Wallace. Write the letter Charles might send to a friend describing his experiences on the journey to find his father. Try to write from Charles Wallace's point of view.

Identification

Find a character on the right who matches the description on the left. Write the letter of the character next to the matching number. Each character is to be used only once.

__ 1. a ten-year old who is building a treehouse with his brother

__ 2. a little boy who hadn't talked at all until he was four

__ 3. a high school student who considers herself "repulsive-looking"

__ 4. a scientist who cooks stew over a bunsen burner

__ 5. She speaks in quotations

__ 6. She was once a star

__ 7. She has no upper teeth and 11 kids

__ 8. a basketball player who compliments Meg's "dreamboat eyes"

__ 9. She doesn't materialize completely because it is tiring

__10. He is a physicist who does top-secret government work

__11. She is gentle, furry, sweet-smelling, has tentacles

__12. the disembodied brain that controls the minds on Camazotz

__13. the Prime Coordinator of Camazotz who hypnotizes Charles

__14. the purple-gowned woman with the crystal ball who unwillingly shows the children the Dark Thing on Earth

A. Meg
B. Charles Wallace
C. Dennys
D. Mrs. Wallace
E. Calvin
F. Mr. Murry
G. Mrs. Whatsit
H. Mrs. Who
I. Mrs. Which
J. the Happy Medium
K. the Man with the Red Eyes
L. It
M. Mrs. O'Keefe
N. Aunt Beast

Multiple Choice

Indicate the letter of the BEST answer.

1. The atmosphere created by the opening scene in the story is best described as
   A. radiant
   B. cheerful
   C. tranquil
   D. threatening

2. When the postmistress asked Meg if she had heard from her father, Meg probably felt
   A. angry with the postmistress for prying
   B. grateful to the postmistress for her concern
   C. curious about how the postmistress knew of her father's absence
   D. suspicious that the postmistress knew Mr. Murry's whereabouts

3. Which of the following describes the twins LEAST well?
   A. athletic
   B. conforming
   C. distinctive
   D. mediocre students

4. Mr. Murry realized that both Meg and Charles would have to adjust to the fact that
   A. they would always be better at reading than writing
   B. they would always score below normal on intelligence tests
   C. they would both develop at their own pace
   D. others would scorn them for being precocious

5. Mrs. Whatsit shocked Mrs. Murry dreadfully by
   A. mentioning that tesseracts exist
   B. ordering her to remove Mrs. Whatsit's boots
   C. asking for Russian caviar
   D. revealing that she knew Mr. Murry's whereabouts

6. Charles Wallace has the uncanny ability to
   A. predict the future
   B. levitate off the floor without moving his legs
   C. speak to Meg without moving his lips
   D. detect what is on Meg's mind

7. Calvin turned up at the haunted house with Meg and Charles because he had
   A. received an invitation in the mail
   B. agreed beforehand to accompany them for moral support
   C. decided to dispel boredom by breaking a few windows
   D. responded to a feeling that he had to go there

8. Mrs. Whatsit took Mrs. Buncombe's sheets because she
   A. needed to "borrow" bedclothes for the beds in the empty house
   B. planned to make ghost costumes for frightening people away
   C. wanted to stir up gossip about the strange tramp
   D. wanted to play a little trick on the gossipy woman

9. The reason Mrs. Who speaks as she does is most like the reason that people might
   A. buy a Valentine card with a printed message instead of making up their own
   B. stammer when they are nervous
   C. be considered to have an "accent" if they come from a different part of the country
   D. speak more clearly and loudly than usual when on stage

10. Mrs. Whatsit took the young people for a ride on her back over Uriel so that they could
    A. see their mother at work in the laboratory
    B. feel what it was like to tesser
    C. see the Dark Thing their father was fighting
    D. hear the beautiful music made by her fellow creatures

11. Suppose a class is given the following assignment: Show in any way you like how two Camazotz neighbors act. Which of the following activities is the best response to that assignment?
    A. Students sing a duet in harmony.
    B. Students stage a loud, angry argument.
    C. Students face each other and move together in mirror-image.
    D. Students dance, one doing a jazz interpretation and the other doing ballet movements.

12. Charles Wallace sat "tucking away" turkey and dressing, although earlier he complained that it tasted like sand. His behavior is most like that of
    A. a child who eats spinach in order to get dessert
    B. a prisoner of war who is brainwashed by the enemy
    C. a young actress who is made up to look like an old woman
    D. a teenager who starts smoking because his friends do

13. Mr. Murry was trapped in the transparent column after
   A. one of his attempts at tessering failed
   B. his captors decided it would keep him from fighting evil
   C. the Happy Medium put him there to keep him safe
   D. the man with the red eyes realized that Mr. Murry might contact Charles

14. If Meg's father had not tessered her when she did, which of the following probably
   would have happened?
   A. Meg would have been absorbed by IT.
   B. Calvin would have shot Aunt Beast.
   C. Meg would have been burned by the Black Thing.
   D. Meg would have knocked down Charles Wallace.

15. Meg has to be the one to rescue Charles Wallace because
   A. Mr. Murry has lost the power to tesser
   B. Calvin has lost his special ability to communicate
   C. The three women cannot find it in their hearts to love the evil IT.
   D. Neither Calvin nor Mr. Murry know and love Charles Wallace as Meg does.

Written Response

I. Analysis

Directions

Select A or B and indicate the letter of the question you decide to answer.

A. Compare this story with another book you have read about the conflict between Good and Evil. Include at least three ways the stories are alike or different.

B. What do you think is the author's theme, or central message? Provide at least three examples from the story to show how the author reveals that theme—directly through the words of certain characters or indirectly through characters' actions. Tell what the events in the story have to do with events in the real world, today.

II. Critical/Creative Thinking

Directions

Select C or D. Indicate the letter of the topic you choose.

C. This book won the Newbery Award for the best piece of children's literature in 1963. Tell why you do or do not feel that it deserves this distinction.

D. Suppose that Mr. Murry decides to tesser to Camazotz a year later to see whether Goodness has made any inroad against Evil. Describe what he learns about the Man with the Red Eyes, IT, and the little boy who had been bouncing the ball differently from the others.

Answer Key

Study Questions

Chapter 1: 1. The dark, stormy weather sets an ominous tone. 2. Meg likes to rough-house, thinks she is ugly, feels mistreated by her teachers, has a temper, loves her little brother, misses her father. 3. They had insulted Charles Wallace, describing him as "dumb." 4. People gossip about Charles Wallace's "low" intelligence and about the fact that Mr. Murry has disappeared—deserted his family for another woman, according to rumor. Meg's mother pays no attention to the gossip, while Meg does. 5. Meg's five-year-old brother didn't speak until he was 4, seems to know what Meg and his mother are feeling and thinking. 6. Both are scientists. 7. Mrs. Whatsit comes during a storm; Charles Wallace met her in the "haunted house." 8. Meg seems irritated with the visitor, mistrustful; she is in a bad mood already and the rumors of the tramp have made her anxious. 9. She turns white when Mrs. Whatsit mentions tesseracts; she doesn't know how the little woman would know of the concept she and her physicist-husband had discussed. 10. She is in trouble with her teacher for being "rude"; her father is missing; people gossip about her brother and father.

Chapter 2: 1. She is a friend of Mrs. Whatsit's—speaks in quotations, wears spectacles. 2. He thinks she should try to conform more, stop day-dreaming at school. 3. Tired from staying up when Mrs. Whatsit visited—she misses a question the teacher asks—the teacher is sarcastic—the class laughs—Meg makes an angry comment—the teacher sends her to the principal. 4. Charles has three reasons for taking Meg to the haunted house: to visit Mrs. Whatsit so Meg can see that the woman can be trusted; to find out more about tesseracts and why Mrs. Whatsit's comment about them shocked Mother; to warn the women that they could be sent to jail for stealing the sheets. 5. Calvin, an upperclassman at Meg's high school felt a "compulsion" to go to the house. 6. She wanted to make ghost costumes for frightening off curious people. 7. They invite Calvin to come to their house for dinner.

Chapter 3: 1. Mrs. Murry is beautiful, bright, a scientist, good-humored, loving; Calvin's mother is a toothless, harried, mother of 11 who doesn't keep track of Calvin. 2. She helps him with his math because her intuitive math skills are excellent. 3. She takes short-cuts, doesn't do things the "right" long way that teachers request. 4. He wants to see what areas she's knowledgeable in; he learns that she is good at math, deficient in geography and English. 5. He feels stifled by his own family, but can relate to Meg's. 6. Mrs. Murry is avoidant; maybe she thinks that the children will worry or be in danger if they know too much. 7. He worked on a classified, dangerous project for the government and traveled a lot; his letters to the family stopped coming; the government informed Mrs. Murry that they would send news as soon as they had it. 8. She has just untangled Mrs. Whatsit's stole and sheets from a tree; Mrs. Who is referring to herself being a lot older and wiser than Mrs. Whatsit.

Chapter 4: 1. Mrs. Which is the third mysterious woman to appear (partially—as a witch-like woman in a peaked hat, with a broomstick); she is authoritative, draws out her words. 2. They tesser the young people to the lovely planet of Uriel so that they can see the Black Thing. 3. She finds it hard to verbalize on her own. 4. golden light, green grass, multicolored flowers, a mountain with birds at its base, delicate butterflies, a crystal river, garden, winged creatures 5. To use a "wrinkle in time" that makes it possible to travel vast distances quickly. 6. She is transformed into a beautiful winged creature with a man's torso. 7. They breathe the flowers when the air thins as they rise. 8. a dark shadow over the Earth marking the forces of Evil 9. so that they will know what they and their father are up against

Chapter 5: 1. They demonstrate tessering; making a "wrinkle in time" enables distances to be traveled in a shorter time, in a fifth dimension. 2. In Alice in Wonderland, only the Cheshire Cat's smile is visible; Mrs. Who often materializes only half-way. 3. She tessers them briefly to a two-dimensional planet where the three-dimensional children experience intolerable pressure. 4. to visit the Happy Medium

---

5. She is a woman in purple robes with a crystal ball (a medium=seer) who prefers things on an even, happy keel and does not like to think about unpleasant matters (keeps a "happy medium"). 6. Under pressure from Mrs. Whatsit, she shows them the Dark Thing on Earth. 7. Like the three women, they are all people who fought for Goodness and Truth.

Chapter 6: 1. She was a star who lost her life while fighting the battle against the Dark Thing. 2. The Happy Medium lets them look into her crystal ball. 3. The Murry children see their mother vent the sorrow she usually keeps from them; Calvin's mother is unkempt, lashing out at her children. 4. sumac, goldenrod, smokestacks of the town, and at the bottom of the hill—a housing development with all houses and lawns exactly alike 5. to Meg—her faults; to Calvin—his ability to communicate; to Charles Wallace—the resilience of childhood 6. her spectacles 7. not to separate; not to use the glasses until necessary; and to Charles—to beware pride and arrogance 8. They all do exactly the same things. 9. Charles retrieves a ball dropped by one little boy and rings the bell; the mother seems frightened and angry at the suggestion that her son is any different from anyone else. 10. His gestures are precise, mechanical; he reveals that only route boys are allowed out at that time and that others need "entrance papers." 11. He had a terrible feeling about the danger inside the CENTRAL Central Intelligence Building.

Chapter 7: 1. She realizes that he is trying to hide his fear behind a joke. 2. His voice is communicated directly to their brains without his lips moving. 3. He will take over all the pain and responsibility of decision-making if they will give themselves up to him. 4. Charles Wallace thinks the man is a robot; the man winces and two men in dark smocks pull Charles Wallace back. 5. He tells them not to look at the man, shows them how to recite something so that they don't fall into his rhythmic recitation. He decides to look at the man and find out who he is. 6. Charles Wallace is becoming hypnotized, but Meg breaks the spell. 7. turkey, stuffing; All enjoy it but Charles, who at that point is the only one to shut his mind entirely to the man's hypnotic suggestions.

Chapter 8: 1. He is enjoying the food; he has opened his mind to the man with the red eyes. 2. He tries to communicate with Charles Wallace and almost breaks the spell. 3. Meg listens for a moment when the man with the red eyes suggests that the three women and Meg's father are untrustworthy, that differences in people create problems. 4. Pain is being used to program him to bounce the ball like other children.

Chapter 9: 1. Longhaired, unshaven, he is trapped in a transparent column. 2. Like Ariel—who was put into a cloven pine by a witch in Shakespeare's The Tempest, Charles Wallace has been trapped by IT. 3. She puts on the spectacles and runs through the column; he reacts in glad surprise, but can't see her. 4. She gives the glasses to her father so that he can use them to rearrange the atoms of the column. 5. Father returns for Meg and tells her to put her arms around his neck. 6. a disembodied brain that controls all thought on Camazotz; She uses her anger to fight the rhythmic squeezing of her brain. 7. She points out that "like" and "equal" are not the same. 8. He suggests she recite the elements of the periodic table.

Chapter 10: 1. Her father tessers her away from IT; his inexperience results in her being numbed by the cold. 2. Meg blames her father for taking her away from Camazotz and deserting Charles Wallace 3. on a planet with gray creatures having four arms and tentacles

Chapter 11: 1. Aunt Beast feeds her, gives her a warm fur, sings her to sleep. 2. Aunt Beast is gray, smells good, covered with fur, walks on two feet, has tentacles; the music is indescribably lovely. 3. They have no eyes; they know what things are, not what they look like. 4. Aunt Beast treats Meg like one of her own babies, long grown; Meg feels like a baby being cared for by an all-loving mother. 5. Someone must go back to Camazotz for Charles Wallace. 6. They hold a meeting to study what is best to do; they do not want to put everyone in danger. 7. Aunt Beast expresses sympathy for Earthlings, who revolve in space alone without communicating with others.

Chapter 12: 1. Mr. Murry hasn't seen much of Charles Wallace and Calvin barely knows him; only Meg has the necessary love for him. 2. She is afraid, but knows she must return. 3. In explaining why it would not be a good thing to be able to see into the future, she compares life to a sonnet—having strict form, but freedom within those confines; in life we have freedom of choice, but must act according to some universal laws. 4. her love 5. She directs her love—something IT does not have—at Charles Wallace and draws him away from IT. 6. Meg and the others are the only ones to have conquered IT and escaped from Camazotz; Meg has learned to face her fear and now realizes the power of love.

Activities

Activity #1: Chart entries will vary, but should reflect these differences between genres: realistic fiction—stories didn't really happen, but characters and situations seem very real; fantasy—highly imaginary characters/situations; science fiction—futuristic, scientifically plausible; historical fiction—untrue stories and characters developed around real events/situations from the past; nonfiction—factual, filled with information; biography—true life stories of real people.

Activity #2: no specific answers

Activity #3: 1. serenity or equanimity-agitation; equanimity-serenity; 2. frenzied-controlled; peremptory-authoritarian; 3. subside-amplify; abdicate-relinquish; 4. alluring-repulsive; impervious-invulnerable; 5. vigorously-half-heartedly; agility-suppleness; 6. embracing-exclusive; belligerent-intractable; 7. prone-supine; inimical-antagonistic

Activity #4: Set #1-metamorphose; 2-gamboled; 3-morass; 4-ephemeral. Student cards will vary.

Activity #5: 1-malignant; 2-furtive; 3-talisman; 4-simultaneously; 5-transition; 6-illuminating; 7-intolerable; 8-aberration; 9-precipitously; 10-propitious;

Activity #6: 1-bland; 2-deviate; 3-annihilate; 4-arrogance; 5-primitive; 6-emanate; 7-bravado; 8-belligerent; 9-pedantic; 10-pinioned; 11-misconception. The travelers end up: at home again.

Activity #7: Message: CLOSE YOUR EYES DO NOT FEAR I AM RETURNING FOR YOU
1-formaldehyde; 2-miasma; 3-angular; 4-placidly; 5-disembodied; 6-inexorable; 7-ominous; 8-insolent; 9-menacing; 10-gibberish; 11-myopic; 12-systole; 13-defer; 14-cerebrum

Activity #8: 1-omnipotent; 2-permeating; 3-trepidation; 4-unadulterated; 5-formidably; 6-fallible; 7-relinquish; 8-jeopardize; 9-ministrations; 10-pungent;
As Meg felt her brain being pulled into IT, she suddenly realized that what SHE HAD THAT IT DID NOT WAS LOVE.

Activities #10 & #11: no specific answers

Activity #12: 1-Sometimes we are guided by how we feel, not what we think; Mrs. Who is defending the fact that the women stole Mrs. Buncombe's sheets because they felt that it was necessary (despite Charles' contention that the action doesn't make sense). 2-An ethical person cannot be kept from doing what is right; Mrs. Who is describing Mr. Murry and the trouble he has gotten into. 3-You can tell a good craftsman by the quality of his work; Mrs. Who is referring to the fact that Mrs. Whatsit is the best at transforming herself, as the beautiful result shows. 4. You can have an intuitive grasp of something without knowing all the facts. Mrs. Who is reminding Charles Wallace not to be arrogant, to realize that he does not know everything. Students' additional quotes will vary.

Activity #13: no specific answers

Activity #14: See page 44 for Crossword Puzzle answers.

Quizzes & Tests

Compehension Quiz (average level):
1-T; 2-F; 3-F; 4-F; 5-F; 6-T; 7-F; 8-T; 9-F; 10-F; 11-F; 12-T; 13-T; 14-F; 15-T

Comprehension Quiz (honors level):
1-They think that he is below normal in intelligence. 2-They are comfortable with it and understand that he will develop at his own pace. 3-She fights with them when they make fun of Charles Wallace. 4-They don't think she is working up to her potential and also think that she is rude. 5-It is rumored that he deserted his family for another woman. 6-He is a physicist. 7-He is from a very large, squabbling family that doesn't pay much attention to him. 8-Both are the "sports" in their families—sensitive, different from others. 9-She tells him she thinks he is handsome. 10-Mrs. Whatsit takes the children to see the Dark Thing from Uriel. 11-She shows them the Dark Thing hovering over the Earth. 12-Father has been fighting the Dark Thing and is in trouble on Camazotz. 13-The people on Camazotz act in unison. 14-He doesn't bounce his ball in rhythm, and drops it. 15-He senses that it is dangerous to go into the building.

Unit Test (average level)
Identification: 1-C; 2-B; 3-A; 4-D; 5-H; 6-G; 7-M; 8-E; 9-I; 10-F; 11-N; 12-L; 13-K; 14-J
Fill-Ins: 1-father; 2-tesseract; 3-government; 4-Whatsit; 5-Who; 6-Which; 7-tramp; 8-storm; 9-tesseracts; 10-Calvin; 11-Camazotz; 12-shadow (thing); 13-crystal ball; 14-shadow; 15-laboratory; 16-O'Keefe; 17-robots; 18-red eyes; 19-Central; 20-hypnotized; 21-spectacles (glasses); 22-column; 23-brain; 24-Mr. Murry;
25-cold; 26-Beast; 27-eyes; 28-Mr. Murry (Father); 29-Camazotz; 30-love
Written Response
A. Details that should be included in the paragraph: They need to find and rescue Mr. Murry. They tesser to Camazotz, walk into town and talk to people for information, locate Mr. Murry and rescue him from the column using the spectacles. B. All are bright, brave, "different;" Charles Wallace has a singular almost telepathic gift; Calvin has a special ability to communicate with other people; Meg has special math/science abilities and is more feisty than the other two. C. Those who argue that the book supports the idea might mention that Mrs. Murry expresses this idea to Meg, and that Meg gets into trouble at school by refusing to conform, and that the Happy Medium is portrayed as a kind, loving being. Those who argue against the idea might mention that striving for a happy medium involves giving in when you should be fighting for what is right. The Happy Medium prefers to ignore Evil—but does nothing to fight it. Mr. Murry would never have fought the Dark Thing, Meg would never have battled IT to save Charles Wallace, if they had decided to walk the middle road. D. Details will vary—tessering to Uriel, Camazotz—being absorbed into IT—being rescued by Meg.

Unit Test (honors level)
Identification: 1-C; 2-B; 3-A; 4-D; 5-H; 6-G; 7-M; 8-E; 9-I; 10-F; 11-N; 12-L; 13-K; 14-J
Multiple Choice: 1-D; 2-A; 3-C; 4-C; 5-A; 6-D; 7-D; 8-B; 9-A; 10-C; 11-C; 12-B; 13-B; 14-A; 15-D
Written Response
A. Responses will vary. Three similarities might include: a journey, one or more "mentors;" a fierce battle with Evil forces. B. Answers will vary. L'Engle seems to be saying that we must tackle the "evils" besetting our planet—war, pollution, oppressive governments—directly, but with love (as shown by Meg at the end, and as stated by the three women when they advise the young people about how to fight IT).
C. Responses should be supported by mention of at least three strengths of the book (e.g., its suspenseful plot, its imaginative settings, the important message it conveys) or three weaknesses.
D. Responses will vary. Some may think that nothing will have changed—but that the boy will now be in sync with the others. Others may feel that the hold over Camazotz has been "cracked" and that there will be more evidence of nonconformity—children playing at different games, adults arranging their gardens differently, etc.

Activity #14:

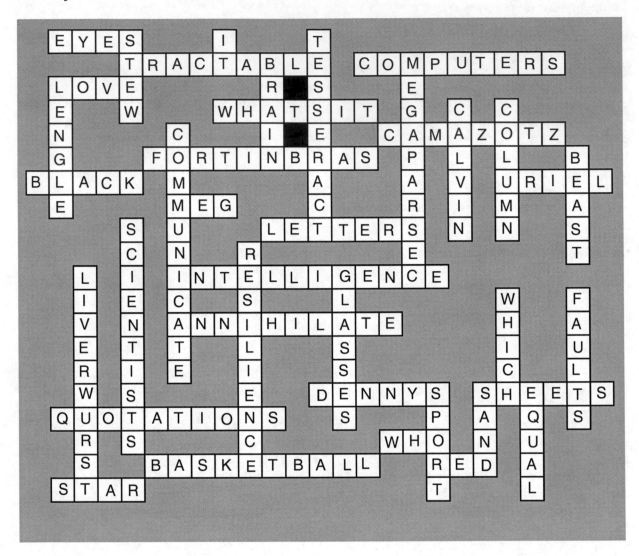